The Windbreaker

By Loren Hackney

All rights reserved

ISBN #: 978-1-958792-08-7

Illustrations by: Korey Woods

This Book Belongs to:

_____

Author Dedication

I would like to dedicate this book to my son, Mason, and my "little brother," Korey for teaching me about all things gross.

Illustrator Dedication

I want to dedicate this to Claudia Keith. Good luck in school!

And, to my son, Sebastian.

After a delicious meal of chili, Mason's belly rumbles and he starts passing gas while outside jumping on his trampoline.

"Mason," says his mom, "stop passing gas!"

The next morning, Mason goes to school and he accidentally farts in his classroom.

Miss Nicely opens her eyes and mouth wide.

"Mason," she says.

His classmates giggle!

He stops farting and gets down to work. He learns math, science, and reads a story to his class.

At lunch, Mason has a peanut butter and jelly sandwich.
He enjoys sharing his veggies and ranch dressing with his friends.

Everyone seems to really like ranch dressing.

On the bus ride home, Mason feels his tummy rumbling again. He is sitting next to his best friend, Shane.

"Hey Mason, pull my finger," says Shane.

"Why?" Mason asks.

"Just do it, please."

Mason pulls Shane's finger and he passes gas! They both burst out laughing.

"Hi, mom!" Mason calls when he comes in the front door.
His mother is cooking and comes out to greet him.
"My...oh my gosh!" she exclaims.
"What is that smell?"
"Say excuse me, Mason!"
Mason mumbles, "Excuse me."
He sulks upstairs.

Mason types *farting* on his tablet. He finds many hilarious videos of people and animals farting.

He snickers and soon he is laughing so hard that he is crying.

His parents hear him laughing and head upstairs.

"What is so funny?"

Mason can't answer because he is laughing so hard.

His mother sighs and rolls her eyes.

"Oh, my goodness!"

His father starts laughing along with him.

"That is hilarious!"

Mason and his father continue to laugh. Mom doesn't think it is that funny and heads downstairs.

"Son, passing gas is funny sometimes, but it is not good to pass gas *all* the time," his father explains.

"Why not?" Mason asks. "Isn't passing gas funny?

His father is embarrassed because he also laughed at the people on the internet.

"Well, passing gas can be funny, but not everywhere and not all the time," he explains.

"Like when we are sitting at church and the choir is about to sing," he says. "You shouldn't fart then. Or when we are at the movie theater and the lights go off. That wouldn't be the time to let one go."

Mason understands,

"Or like when we are at the planetarium and the stars come out?"

"Yes," his father says.

"Or at the dinner table when I ask mommy to pass the mashed potatoes?" Mason asks.

"Exactly!" says his father.

Mason sits and thinks.

"So, when is a good time to fart?" he asks.

His father thinks and says, "When you are with your friends or when you are at the amusement park. The bathroom is the best place to fart," he says.

"Another thing," he adds. "The proper word for it is passing gas."

"Passing gas? Like gas for a car?" he asks.

"No, gas is in your tummy. It is all the leftover yucky stuff. That's why farts smell so bad," says dad.

That night at dinner, Mason felt like he had to *pass gas*.

"Excuse me, may I go to the bathroom?" he asked.

When he got up to go to the bathroom, he smiled at his father and his father gives him a big thumbs up sign!

On Saturday, the soccer van came around to pick up Mason. He had a healthy breakfast of raisin bran and milk to give him energy to play well.

He was in the outfield waiting to get into the game when he felt his tummy rumbling again!

"Uh oh!"

He started to sweat.

"Coach!"
Oh my gosh, he thought,
the coach is still a ways away
and I feel it coming!

Rrrrriiiippp!

Mason's hands made a swiping motion around his middle when the coach finally came up to him.

"Yeah, buddy. What's up?"

Mason's face flushed!

"I had to pass gas, but now I don't"

The coach patted Mason on the back.

"That's okay buddy, you did it at the right time.

No one is around!"

**He exhaled and wiped the sweat from his brow...
and smiled!**

The End